The SUN is on
Poetry & Ideas

Lindamichellebaron

6th Edition

poetry by Lindamichellebaron
revised to include creative activities
Introduction by Ruby Dee

ISBN-13: 978-0-940938-05-2
ISBN-10: 0-940938-05-7
The Sun Is On, 6th Edition

To order:
HARLIN JACQUE PUBLICATIONS
PO Box 336
Garden City, NY 11530
Tel: 516-489-0120
Fax: 516-292-9120
harlinjacquepub@aol.com
www.lindamichellebaron.com

COVER AND BOOK DESIGN: RANEE CHUNG

For Grown-Ups ...... Introduction by Ruby Dee 4

From Me To You .... (a brief autobiography from and about the author) 5

The Sun is On You 8

If I Were Music   Me, Myself, and I ! 10

The Love Maker   Show Your Love ! 12

When I Grow Up   Upside Down and Inside Out ! 14

Real True Haiku and A Path to Math ...Please   Magic Math Problems 16

Better Not "Badder"   Pictures of "Badder" and Better 18

Go Away   Letter from the Heart 20

Well Done (Part I)   Look Who's Talking ! 22

Well Done (Part II)   A Thousand Thanks

A Natural Fit   Talking Shapes 26

A Natural Fit   Dear Diary

The Lonely Shoe   Turning Loneliness Around 30

Growing Like a Weed   Blossoming All Along the Way 32

A Flower   Directions for Growing Me ! 34

Even Weeds Have Needs   That Special Someone 36

And Be Glad and Brownish-Sandy Cotton Candy   Blue Ribbon Prize 38

Hair Tears   No More Tears 40

Praying   Talking to Myself 42

Hair Prayer   Holiday Picture 44

Hair Prayer   Make a Wish

It Hurts   The Wonderful Word Machine 48

All That Makes Me So Unique   I'm Celebrating Me ! 50

The Way to Start the Day   Three Cheers for You ! 52

Jumping Double Dutch   Jump So High I'll Catch My Star ! 54

Little Herman   You Are My Sunshine 56

Daddy's Little Girl   Love Makes a Family 58

Daddy's Little Girl   Recipe for Love

Hugs and Kisses   GirlStuff ! BoyStuff ! 62

I'll Try and Growing Equation   Life Equations 64

On A Limb   Talking to an Apple 66

On A Limb   Talking to Yourself

Just Push   My Key to Knowledge 70

Ghetto-ites   Pride Poem 72

Homesick   Advice for Harold 74

Homesick   Imagination Station

Halloween Madness   The Beauty of Differences 78

Blackness Is   The Beauty in Me 82

Poetry Is Me   Wonder Word 84

Stranded...Marooned   The Other Side of the Moon 86

Idea Sitting and In Other Words   Pick Up Your Pencil! 88

Spelling Blues   Sing Out ! 90

A World to Read   Opening Doors 92

Much, Much More...   I Am A Poem ! 94

Poetic License ... Bonus Page 96

Introduction

For Grown Ups
by Ruby Dee

You can sense immediately in THE SUN IS ON that Lindamichellebaron has been looking deep into the eyes, the faces, the hearts and minds of young and not so young people for a long time. She has found some unformed questions, some unexposed hurts and some unexpressed joys. When she realized that she'd never get around to drying all the tears, bandaging all the wounds, hugging away all the hurts, and celebrating all the overlooked joys; she decided to leave presents around. Anyone needing an explanation or an affirmation or a surprise could just help themselves. Armed with a wide open, available literary style, she went back into her own childhood, and her own adulthood, she remembered where the growing-up gaps for a lot of us were. Then she filled them with deep rhythms that surfaced in light and easy-to-read poems.

I especially like, what I call, the parable poems. An old toothbrush is consoled in "Well Done." There is a delightful warning against impatience to a young green apple on an apple tree in "On A Limb." "Even Weeds Have Needs" says that even if I'm not a super special kind of person, I need love and tending. "Talk to me" and help me be "Better Not Badder," is the theme of another poem. She also says out loud what probably goes on in the minds of some little Black girls dealing with hair that is hard to comb. Linked with the fun of "Halloween Madness" are thoughts on group identity and differences within the group. If I had to choose a favorite it might well be the lyrical, joyous and loving "Daddy's Little Girl." The inspiration for all these poems are ideas that profoundly need to be expressed.

This book is a must for adults who are involved with keeping our youngsters' minds together and informed.

In each one of the offerings in THE SUN IS ON is a lesson-gem sure to stimulate plenty of interaction among children of all ages. I believe many people will say, "Read it out loud! Listen to this! Let's read it to music!" THE SUN IS ON is like having a good picture on the front page of yourself.

From ME To YOU

*from the child in me
to the child in you...*

*"I have a cousin named Gerard,
I think his ears are very odd..."*

Those words may not be an example of poetic genius, but they are the first lines of poetry I ever wrote. I was about six years old. My mother read them to anyone who called or visited us. My father shared them with the members of his congregation. My dog, Pogo, wagged his stub of a tail. Gerard, my cousin, started wearing his hair long enough to cover his ears. So what if my brother, Chip, couldn't have cared less. I kept writing. "My brother is a pest. He's worse than all the rest." and "I love my mother. She's better than any other."

My teachers smiled and encouraged me, even though my poems were exactly like a million other poems written by children my age. Thank goodness, I didn't know it at the time. So, I wrote all through elementary school. I'd ask my classmates, "You want to hear my new poem?" "No," they'd answer. I'd laugh a bit and read it to them anyway. I found out later that most of them only listened because my best friend and guardian angel, Eileen, threatened to beat up anyone who didn't listen.

When Eileen wasn't around, writing kept me out of fights. When the kids teased me about my hair (mop top), or my complexion, or what I wore, or maybe even my dimple (the hole in the side of my face), I would write them out of existence. "Take that... and that...you...you... What rhymes with..."

By the time I arrived in Junior High School 59, in Queens, I considered myself a real poet. I discovered Edgar Allen Poe and James Clifton Morris. I loved the author, Poe, for his deep writings. I memorized "The Raven" and tried to copy the style and rhyming pattern. Thanks to his influence and some of the other authors I read during that time, most of my poetry was about death and depression. For example:

> The wintry night is the cause of my fright
> the door of destiny is ajar
> the breath of death is the caller of my soul
> a voice from the heavens afar.

I also loved Mr. Morris, my teacher, and a published poet. He was a great educator. He loved literature and young people. He told the worst puns in the world. For example, "What's a metaphor?" The answer? "Cows." (You'll get it, eventually.) But he took my writing seriously. He showed me how to make my writing better. I didn't always agree, but I learned.

Sometimes, I wrote about mushy, boy and girl love. I didn't even have a boyfriend. How would I know about that stuff? But that didn't matter to me. It seemed like a good topic to write about, so I wrote about it.

Eventually, I found my own creative voice. In Springfield Gardens High School, I finally decided I didn't have to write like somebody else. I could be me. The poetry of Langston Hughes helped me to make this important discovery. He wrote about people, and music, and the upside of life. When he wrote about the downside of living, he wrote from his experience, with his own style.

So, more and more of who I am began to come out in my poetry. I enjoy life and people and music, too. So my poetry became more "me." Some people say that "me" comes from an oral tradition. I think they mean that people really get more of the feelings and rhythms I put into my poetry when they hear it read out-loud. That's one of the reasons why my husband, Harold Dudley, and I developed an audio cassette version of THE

SUN IS ON. We wanted you to hear the poems being read aloud. But you can read this book out-loud to yourself and others. Please do. Add your own expressions, your own feelings, and your own rhythms as you read them.

I continue to write about the joys of life. And the love I write about is not "kissy, huggy" love, but "caring about others" love. I am motivated to write just by experiencing life, people, and books. Reading fills me with thoughts, of new ways of looking, seeing and expressing myself, and new ideas using my own style.

Believe it or not, some of the poems in THE SUN IS ON were written when I was in high school: "On A Limb," "The Lonely Shoe," "Well Done... Part 1," and "A Natural Fit." I wrote some of them when I majored in education at New York University: "Blackness Is," "Hair Prayer," and "Hair Tears." Some of the others were sparked by my teaching experience in Public School 21, in Brooklyn: "Ghetto-ites," "Growing Equation," "I'll Try," "The Love Maker," "Halloween Madness," and "Praying."

When I taught, I spiced every subject with poetry and literature. We read, recited, memorized and dramatized the written word. We chanted and clapped to rhythms and rhymes every morning. The children even made up their own. "I feel good... like I should," "Glad to say... happy _____ " (insert the day of the week).

It doesn't really matter when I wrote these poems. Most of what you'll read in this book is written from the child in me. I haven't grown up yet, even though some young people think I'm a hundred years old. Some people think I'm dead, because I'm in a book. Well, as long as I'm here, I don't plan to get old. I hope my poetry helps to keep you young, and filled with the joy of life, too. That's probably why I named this book after the words my nephew, Herman, smiled out many years ago, " *The* sun is on!"

You'll find a poetic license in the back of this book, to help remind you to keep writing. I hope you use it to help free yourself to write more and more and...

> *Even when I sleep my thoughts won't keep.*
> *Let me out, thoughts shout from inside my head.*
> *So I guide them in with paper and pen.*
> *I plan to guide some more in so I can visit again.*

Not only do I love writing poetry, I also love reading other writers' poems. When I read a new poem, I try to find a "path" into it—like someone traveling to a new place. How do I do that? I read the poem carefully. I say it out loud and listen to its own special music. I think about how it connects to my own feelings, my own thoughts—my own life ! And, like any good traveler, I choose a "souvenir" to take away with me. How? I think about what I like most about the poem—it could be the title, a phrase, a word, the way the poem looks on the page, the way it sounds, the way it affects my heart and brain, or anything else. And then I "pack" my souvenir in the "suitcase" of my memory—so I will always have it with me.
Now I invite you to find your path into my poems. Use the activity that follows each poem as a map to help you find your way. Bon voyage !

Linda Michelle Baron

The Sun Is On You

Use the graphic organizers.
They can help you think through the story of you. Draw or write your entries.
Share your thoughts with friends and family members.

(A) Create a spider web of your thoughts, phrases, and beliefs about you.

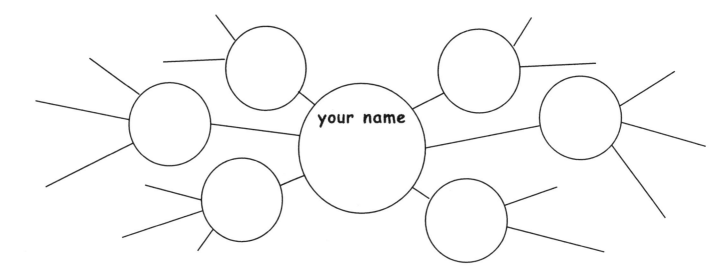

your name

(B) Create your personal timeline. Include experiences, people, places, and things.

your past	your present	your future

Ⓒ Fill in this circle with words, phrases, and quotes about you.

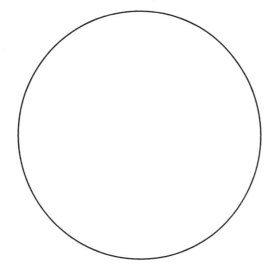

Ⓓ

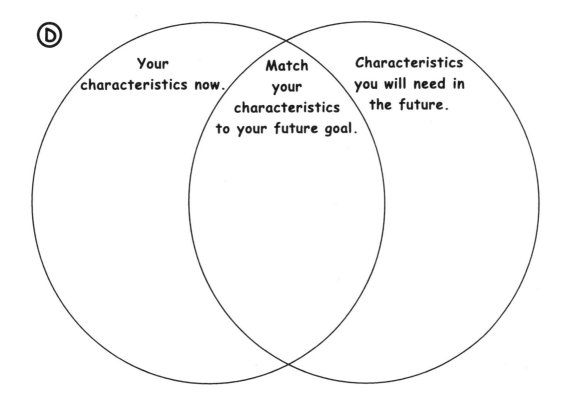

Your characteristics now.

Match your characteristics to your future goal.

Characteristics you will need in the future.

If I Were Music

If I were music
I'd be jazz
So real you'd feel my pure
pizzazz!

Snazzy, jazzy . . . boiling ice
I'd never play the same way twice

When He made me
God closed his eyes
Heard the music
And improvised!!!

Me, Myself, and I! [If I Were Music]

The poet says she'd be jazz ... if she were music.
What would you be?

If I were music

> I'd be
>> because

If I were a color

> I'd be
>> because

If I were an animal

> I'd be
>> because

If I were a day of the week

> I'd be
>> because

Now create a collage that SHOWS who you are. Cut out
pictures, photographs, and words from magazines,
newspapers, and catalogs. Arrange them in a design that
reveals the real you! Paste the elements on a sheet of paper.
Add your own artwork. And, of course, place your name
prominently in your me-myself-and-I creation.

THE LOVE MAKER

I'm a Sunday to Saturday Santa,
and I'm not any "Claus."
I'm everybody's happy...
because I'm a topsy turvy, upsy daisy
love person.

Sometimes, I'm as quiet as a well worn sneaker.
I can be love without making a squeaker.
Sometimes, I'm as loud as a GIANT'S SHAKER.
I can be anything to anyone,
because I am a love maker.

If you don't see me, you can still tell I'm here.
When I walk in, you feel love appear.
I'm "Happy Holidays" three hundred
sixty-five days a year.

Don't look for me in Macy's, Gimbles'* or Gertz*
You won't find me with toys or in children's wear
near shirts or with skirts.

But,
you can find me in a kiss, in a kind word,
in a hug or a smile...
Just living and being love...
I am a L O V I N G child.

If you want to see me,
there's no need for surprise.
If you're looking for me, just open your eyes.
You'll see there's nobody new.
Just see me
in you.

*These were department stores.

Show Your ♥!

Think of the many ways you can show caring, kindness, and love to others.

How could you show your caring, kindness, and love ...

in a quiet way?

in a noisy way?

in a little way?

in a big way?

in an invisible way?

in a funny way?

How do you like others to show their caring, kindness, and love to you?

13

WHEN I GROW UP

When I grow up, I'll be a clown.
Flop my face up... and flop my face down...
No one will say, "Quit clowning around,"
when I grow up and be a clown.

I'll act silly, stupid, dumb, insane.
I'll use my funny bone and rest my brain.
No one will call me immature.
They'll laugh and call me back for more.

When I grow up and be a clown,
I'll turn the school rules upside down.
If you act silly and start to laugh,
I'll cut your ticket price in half.

If you fold your hands, and sit quiet and nice,
you'll pay two times the regular price.
And if you look like you're a teacher,
I'll seat you in the furthest bleacher.

They'll beg to see me in every town...
The Fun-tabulous!
Fabulous!
Funny Face Clown...

14

Upside Down and Inside Out!

Rules! Rules! Rules! Everyday you follow town and city rules, school rules, and home rules. But suppose you could turn the rules upside down and inside out?

What would your new rules be? Write three rules just the way you'd like them. (Draw your ideas instead, if you'd like.)

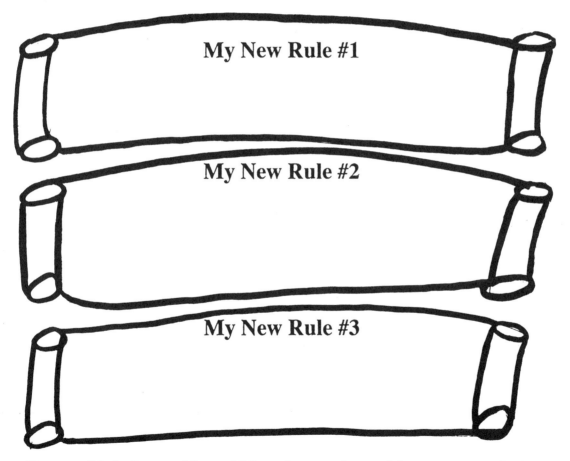

My New Rule #1

My New Rule #2

My New Rule #3

Do you think the world would be a better place with your new rules? Tell why or why not.

REAL TRUE HAIKU...

I had some trouble
learning how to multiply...
trouble never did.

A PATH TO MATH...PLEASE!

Math isn't easy.
I don't care what they say.
I'm going to close my eyes
and subtract it away . . .
Divide what's left..
Watch it disappear.
Sure hope this problem
is divisible by fear.

5 x6 =!

0 x 5 = ?

4

?

#

#

Ahah!

Magic Math Problems

Here are some math problems you'll never find in your math book. Let your imagination go wild as you answer each one.

+ ADDITION
List three ways you could ADD happiness to the lives of the people you love.
1.
2.
3.

- SUBTRACTION
List three things you could SUBTRACT from your life that would make you a happier or better person.
1.
2.
3.

× MULTIPLICATION
List three of your skills or talents that you could MULTIPLY by working a little harder.
1.
2.
3.

÷ DIVISION
List three ways you could DIVIDE up your love and energy to share more with others.
1.
2.
3.

BETTER NOT "BADDER"

Sometimes I wish
I could fold myself
between two pieces of bread
and gobble myself away,
'til there's no more.

That's how bad I feel, sometimes.
Especially when I do something
really, really bad.

That's when I want you
to do something
to help me be better —
not "badder" next time.

That's when I want you
to talk *with* me, not to the air,
or other people.

That's when I need
to hear you say something other than...
"I just don't know what to do with this child!"

Pictures of "Badder" and "Better"

Draw a "badder" picture or write a "badder" poem. Express what you feel like inside when you do something really, really bad.

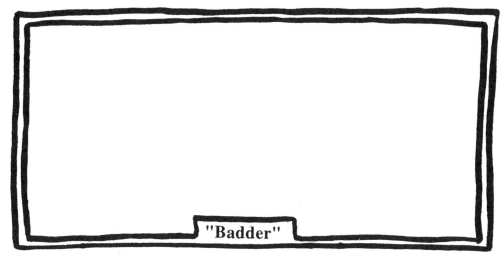

Draw a "better" picture or write a "better" poem. Express what you feel like inside when someone forgives you or says kind words to you after you've done something really, really bad.

GO AWAY

Somehow I'm always
                    in the way.
I'm always sent somewhere
                    to play.
Or told to go and watch TV.

Is it them?
                    Or is it me?

Letter from the Heart

Write a letter to the little girl. Tell her something that will make her feel better. Maybe you can share with her a time when you felt the same way. Maybe you can give her good advice to feel better.

If you'd like, write your letter as a poem. Or create a drawing that would make the little girl feel better.

Dear Little Girl,

Sincerely,

WELL DONE... PART I

Toothbrushes on the sink,
expecting to be used,
discussing their age old problem
of having been abused.

One was missing bristles
and no one seemed to care,
if the shabby toothbrush
went without repair.

Another, cracked and worn,
looking rather bad,
spent his time discussing
the beauty he once had.

The rubber tip on one,
was just an empty space.
No one thought to put
a new tip in its place.

They were so unhappy
their thoughts turned into tears.
They remembered all
they lost throughout the years.

The sink sat silently and listened,
and then had this to say
to her disgruntled friends
who spoke of their dismay.

*"You each have whitened teeth
and dueled with tooth decay.
You served humanity
every single day.*

*Your work will be remembered
whenever people smile.
Your hard work will be remembered
for a very long while.*

*You should try to remember
how much you really won.
You have the satisfaction of knowing
you did your job...
'Well Done.'"*

WELL DONE... PART II

Some shook their bristles and said,
"Who asked her to think?"
Some didn't hear one word
spoken by Ms. Sink.

Some of the others heard
and could tell Sink was sincere,
but felt the problem went beyond
their outward disrepair.

They had indeed worked hard
and with a sense of pride,
but they couldn't excuse being overused,
and carelessly cast aside.

Mirror reflected,
"If you'd been rinsed and stored,
protected not just used and ignored,
you'd feel better about life's wear and tear
if they'd shown appreciation,
acted like they cared."

The toothbrushes looked at Mirror,
smudged and splattered,
and knew how Mirror understood
what really mattered.

They all applauded the Mirror, shouting,
"That's it! That's it!... Exactly!"
"I know," was all that Mirror said,
far from matter of factly.

Look Who's Talking!

Imagine that your belongings could talk. What would they say about the way you treat them?

My toothbrush:

My shoes:

My schoolbooks:

My pencil or pen:

My favorite belonging:

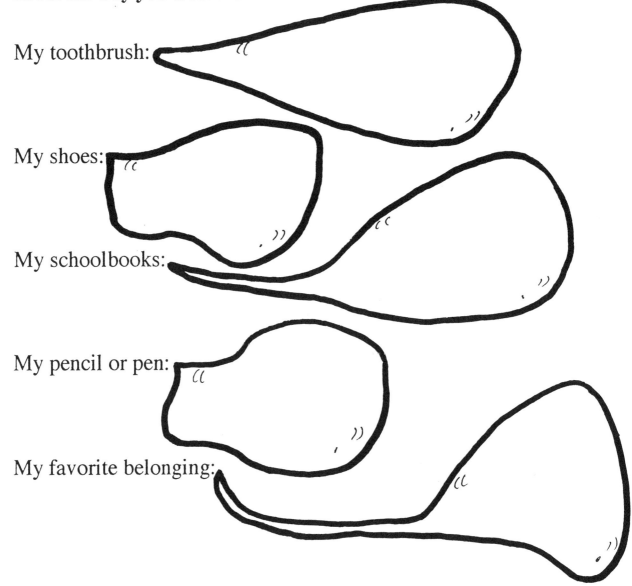

A Thousand Thanks

Choose one of the following: your toothbrush, shoes, schoolbooks, pencil or pen, or favorite belonging. Then write a thank-you note to it to express your appreciation. If you'd like, write your note as a poem.

Dear

Sincerely,

Now write a thank-you note to someone you know. Express your appreciation for something the person has done for you.

Dear

Sincerely,

A Natural Fit

There once was a square
who seldom got anywhere,
for try as she would
she just never could
fit in.

Each space she could find
was all the wrong kind
as she pushed to belong,
with her choice always wrong
each time.

The day that she saw
a circular door,
she tried as she would,
but just never could
fit in.

A rectangle was next
and almost annexed,
but two sides were too tall,
two others too small
for her.

One day something new
came into view,
differently framed,
and peculiarly named
triangle.

But the figure she spied,
was minus one side.
So try as she would
she still never could
fit in.

She finally succeeded,
in finding the space that she needed.
To her happy surprise
it had four sides the same size
for her.

Now she's the happiest square
you can ever find anywhere.
She's the square that could
and finally would
fit in.

Talking Shapes

If the shapes in the poem "A Natural Fit" could speak, what would they say? Let your imagination go wild!

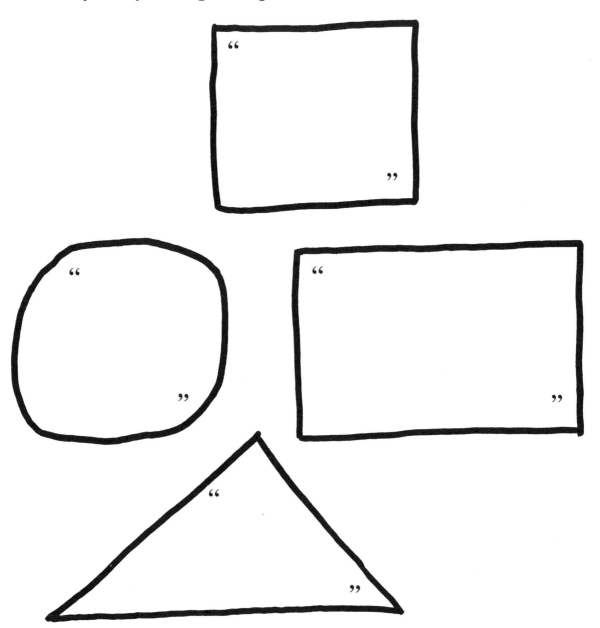

Dear Diary

Imagine you are the square in "A Natural Fit." Write an entry in your diary. Tell what it felt like "to fit in" at last.

Dear Diary,

Have you ever felt as if you didn't "fit in"? What advice would you give to someone who was feeling that way?

The Lonely Shoe

Walking to and fro,
without a place to go...
A shoe.

Looking for his twin,
a relative or kin...
He looks.

It seems a little queer,
to see the little dear
walking to and fro,
without a place to go...
A shoe
            without
                        a foot.

Turning Loneliness Around

What does loneliness feel like to you? Add your ideas to the wheel.

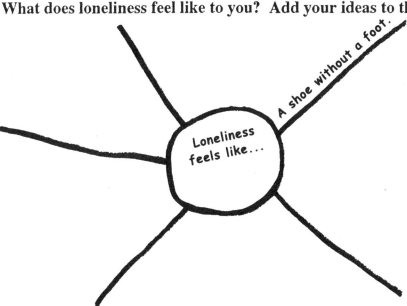

How can you help yourself when you're feeling lonely? Add your ideas to this wheel.

Growing Like a Weed

I don't grow like no weed!
No indeed!
I just blossom
quick!

Blossoming All Along the Way

Do you "blossom quick" like the poet? Or do you "blossom slow"?
Whether you're quick or slow—you grow, learn, and achieve your whole
life long! In the petals of the flower, record some of the ways you've
blossomed.

Something I
learned today:

Something I
learned yesterday:

Something I did
that I'm proud of:

My Name:

How I helped
someone:

My favorite
achievement:

My greatest
strength:

A Flower

I think some kids
come here knowing everything already . . .
don't need no help.
Not me!
I need nurturing.
Some kind, caring hands helping me.

Some kids
(I say they weeds)
don't need nothing.
Can know and do everything
without no help.
Popping up with right answers
without no nurturing.
Not me!

I need time and care,
'cause a flower don't just pop up.
I need time and care,
'cause a flower has to be . . .
    petted by the sun,
    fed by the earth,
    refreshed by the rain
    and protected by The Maker . . .
like me.
'Cause I ain't no weed,
like some kids
is!!!

[A Flower]

Directions for Growing Me!

Complete this "gardener's guide" to express who you are. Write poems or draw pictures if you like.

Directions for Growing Me

I'm a human flower called: _____

Here's what I look and feel like today:

Here's what I'll look and feel like when I'm all grown up:

I grow best when ... (Check as many as you like.)
- ☐ **I have lots of friends around me.**
- ☐ **I have one good friend.**
- ☐ **I have lots of time alone.**
- ☐ **I have just a little time alone.**
- ☐ **People treat me the way I treat them.**
- ☐ **I can show my feelings to the people around me.**
- ☐ **I keep my feelings to myself.**
- ☐ **People treat me with patience and kindness.**

Here are other conditions that help me grow best.

Even Weeds
Have Needs

Even weeds have needs, you know.
Don't make me creep through cracks,
or race for space to grow.

Even weeds have needs, although,
I've been known to survive on dried up rain
and left over sun.

Even weeds have needs, you know.
A dandelion can die in careless hands,
and under misplaced feet.

Even weeds have needs, you know.
And this weed needs a great big garden,
with a gardener who's not afraid
to let me grow.

That Special Someone

The weed in the poem wants "a gardener who's not afraid to let me grow." We all have "gardeners" in our lives who help us learn, understand, and grow. These gardeners might be favorite teachers or coaches or people at church or relatives or friends. Think about the gardeners in your life and how you could be a gardener to somebody else.

My Life Garden

The "gardener" in my life is:
_____ .

This person has helped me grow in the following ways:

Other People's Life Gardens

I could be a "gardener" in the life of:
_____ .

Here's how I could help that person grow:

And Be Glad

If I grow up
"just like my dad"
the hair I have,
will be "the hair I had"

So,
coarse or thin...
styled "out" or "in"...
called "good" or "bad"
I'll keep what I got...
and be glad!

Brownish-Sandy Cotton Candy

My hair is cotton –
cotton candy.
Soft, tight curls —
but brownish –
sandy.

I fluff it up.
It stays in place.
Soft, fluffed, short
hair
hugs my face.

All hugged up
I have to grin.
Hair that hugs me —
outside in.

Blue Ribbon Prize

Think about the things that you like about yourself and wouldn't ever want to change. (They can be on the outside or on the inside!) Choose one. Then give yourself a blue ribbon prize for it! Express yourself as you fill in the ribbon. Write or draw or create a poem.

I award this Blue Ribbon Prize to myself, _____.
(your name)

The thing I am most proud of about myself:

Here's why it deserves the prize:

Here are some other things I like about myself:

I'm going to work on these things so I can award myself another blue ribbon:

HAIR TEARS

...And a little girl still prays...
because her hair won't grow.

Even though her mommy
stopped straightening it,
and "natural" is beautiful,
she cries,
because people keep calling her,
"him"

Even though she prays...
beautiful people, and other people
still say, "What a nice little boy!"
to her mother,
when she wears pants to play in,
or to her teacher,
when she sits behind a desk,
where dresses aren't seen.
And she knows her mommy and daddy
love her,
but she still prays
for her hair to grow,
so that she can play through one morning...
without being called
                              "he"

No More Tears

Imagine you could talk to the little girl in the poem and dry her tears. Make her feel better by telling her about a problem you once had. Then tell her how you solved the problem.

Create a "photo album" to show her what you're talking about. Make a "snapshot" of the problem and a "snapshot" of the solution. Use words and drawings to create your snapshots.

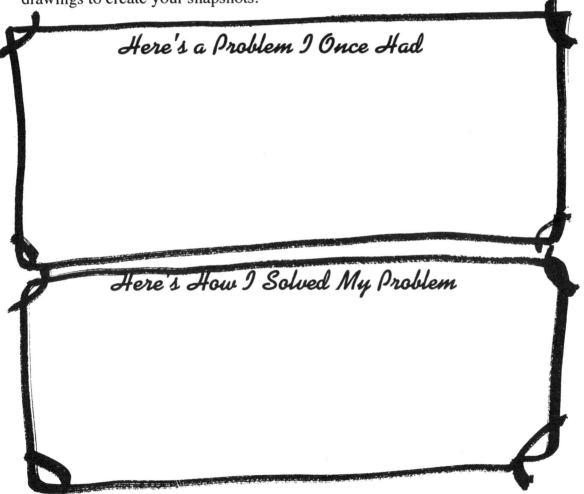

Here's a Problem I Once Had

Here's How I Solved My Problem

Praying

"Praying..."
the little girl said,

"Is when you close your eyes... and fold your hands like this

...and talk to yourself."

Talking to Myself

Stop and listen to your heart! Write what it is saying to you.

What my ♥
is saying to me …

HAIR PRAYER

Now I lay me down to sleep, I...
Excuse me Lord, for not going on,
but You know what tomorrow is...
Christmas Eve.
That means my hair has to be washed,
combed out and straightened
early tomorrow morning.

I just thought I'd ask if You
could make my hair, what they call "good"
just until after Christmas.
I don't think I can sit through my mother
slowly burning me to death
with that   **big**
           hot
           iron
           comb
after she has already tried to pull my head off
by my tangles.

If You can't do that,
maybe You could just give my mother a few dollars,
so she can send me to the hairdresser.

I won't mind wearing it the way it is,
if You make Mommy promise
she won't ship me off to Africa,
or any place else.
Just tell her You love me the way I am.

It's Your birthday
and Your mother didn't even press her hair
when You were born.
And You had all of those visitors.

The only ones coming to visit us Christmas
are my grandparents.
They've seen my hair like this before.
Anyway, it's partly their fault.

If that's too hard,
maybe you could just
turn me into a boy.

I guess I'll find out tomorrow,
after I get my hair washed,
but if Your will and my will
are the same . . .
may Our will be done.
Happy Birthday, Lord.
AMEN.

Holiday Picture

Christmas for the girl in the poem is wonderful and terrible. It's wonderful because it's a joyful holiday. It's terrible because her mother is forcing her to sit through the painful process of getting her hair done.

Think about one of your favorite holidays. Then create a picture that shows what it's like in your family. Show the joys and the woes. Create your "holiday picture" with words or drawings or both.

Make a Wish

The girl in the poem says a "hair prayer." Some people say that a prayer is a wish your heart makes. Think about some wishes you might like to make for yourself and others. Express yourself in words, poems, or drawings.

♥A wish for me:

♥A wish for someone in my family:

♥A wish for a friend:

♥A wish for my school:

♥A wish for my town:

♥A wish for the world:

IT HURTS

Sometimes their words
smash my brain like rain
beating cement
and that's why I cry.

Even though I know
that only sticks and stones
crack bones,
sometimes their words smash rain
through cracks to my brain,
and I can feel it all seep
deep inside . . .
and it hurts.

That's why I cry.

The Wonderful Word Machine

Words can hurt—like the poem says. And words can heal. We can't stop others from saying terrible words to us. But we can remember that good, kind, sparkling words make the world a better place.

Turn the words that hurt into words that heal and help. Pick up your pen or pencil and turn on the Wonderful Word Machine!

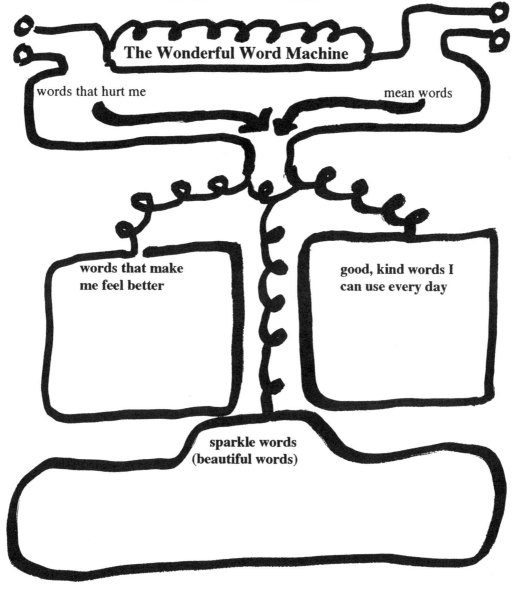

The Wonderful Word Machine

words that hurt me

mean words

**words that make
me feel better**

**good, kind words I
can use every day**

**sparkle words
(beautiful words)**

ALL THAT MAKES ME SO UNIQUE

When they used to tease me,
or when they'd laugh or stare,
I'd shut my eyes real tight
and pretend I wasn't there.

I tried to be extra good.
I thought no one would see
the part of me that's different,
if I were different, quietly.

I didn't look in mirrors.
I didn't want to hear or see
the mirrored differences
shouting back at me.

I really wanted "same-ness"
Put "different" on a shelf...
Until my friend helped show me
the wonder of myself.

My friend said to imagine
a world with everything the same.
Everything monotonously
all the same.... the same... the same.

The world... an outline drawing...
with no specifics painted in...
not even shades of music...
a world without reason to spin.

Of course, we each are different.
We each should celebrate
the colors, curves, dimensions
that we each radiate.

Now, I celebrate my differences...
All that makes me so unique.
Why let others define me,
when I can be my own critique?

I'm Celebrating Me!

Imagine you're having a party to celebrate you! Complete this party invitation. Tell about the "colors, curves, and dimensions" that you radiate.

Party Time!

You are invited to a party celebrating me!

My name:_____

Day:_____ **Place:**_____
     (your favorite day of the week)   (your favorite place)

Time:_____
     (your favorite time of the year and favorite time of the day)

The decorations are going to be _____.
                       (your favorite color)

To express who I am, the decorations will look like this: _____

_____.

At my party, we're going to celebrate all the ways I'm special:

Everybody knows I'm special in this way:

Nobody knows–but me!–that I'm special in this way:

Here's a way I'd like to be special some day:

Here's my plan for how I'm going to achieve that goal:

Oh—and one more thing! Make a list of a few special people you'd be sure to invite to your party. Explain why each one is on your "special list."

The Way to Start the Day

This is the way... **hey!** we start the day... **hey!**

We get the knowledge... **hey!** to go to college... **hey!**

We won't stop there... **hey!** go anywhere... **hey!**

We work and smile... **hey!** cause that's our style... **hey!**

We love each other... **hey!** help one another... **hey!**

There's nothing to it... **hey!** just have to do it... **hey!**

This is the way... **hey!** we start the day... **hey!**

'Cause we "don't play"... **hey!**

Now, what you say... **hey!!!**

Three Cheers for You!

The poem "The Way to Start the Day" is a cheer. It's a cheer that says, "I can do great things!" Write your own three cheers to keep yourself going strong all day long! Express your cheers as poems if you like.

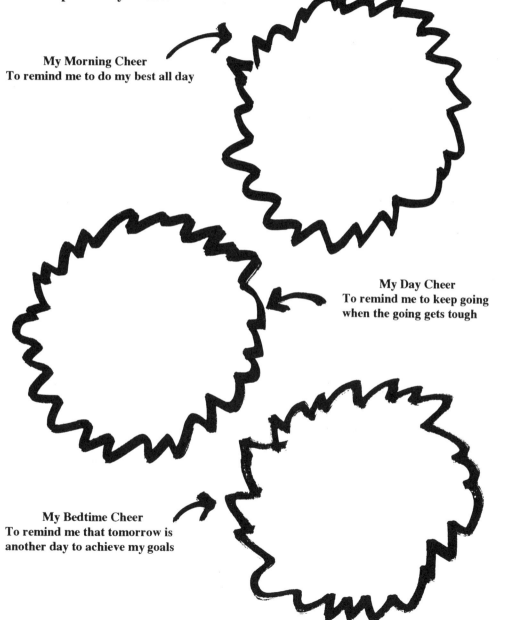

My Morning Cheer
To remind me to do my best all day

My Day Cheer
To remind me to keep going
when the going gets tough

My Bedtime Cheer
To remind me that tomorrow is
another day to achieve my goals

Jumping Double Dutch

We can double dutch turn,
turning jumps into a dance.
Our steps are serious.
We don't make them up by chance.

Some think jumping is a game.
Jumping rope is more than that.
Watch us tumble, fast and agile,
jumping sidewalk acrobats.

We can double dutch dance.
We can double dutch sing.
We can double dutch do about anything.

Double ten, twenty, thirty...
keeping count to keep the beat.
If you want to see us miss, if I were you,
I'd take a seat.

Jump So High I'll Catch My Star!

The poem "Jumping Double Dutch" says you can do anything you put your mind to.
Write about your special talent and how you'll use it to catch your star.
Remember—there are many kinds of talents.

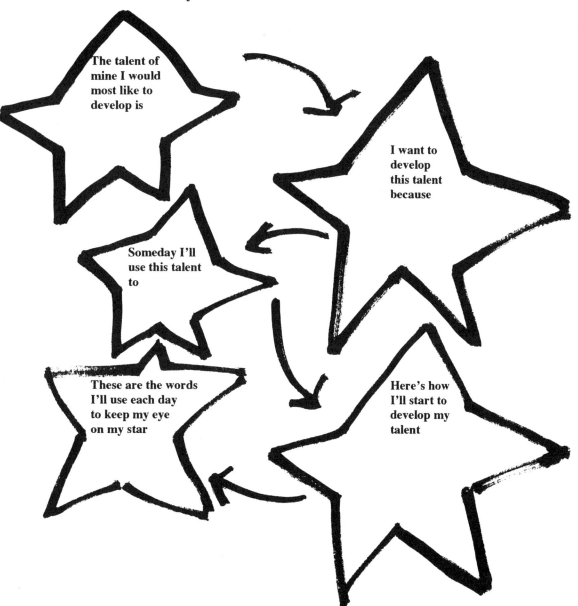

The talent of mine I would most like to develop is

I want to develop this talent because

Someday I'll use this talent to

These are the words I'll use each day to keep my eye on my star

Here's how I'll start to develop my talent

Little Herman

First thing you did was smile
and kiss out the words,
"Good morning, the sun is on."
Don't you know you turned it on
when you smiled yourself awake ?

Bet your daddy caught some of that sun
last time you two went fishing,
and wrapped it around your little body.
So now,
when you start to wake up the morning
with that smile of yours,
some sun pops out too
to cover up any little mischief
that just happens to wake up with you
when *"the sun is on"*.

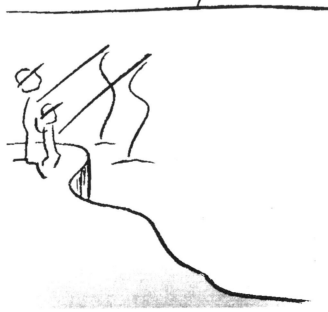

You Are My Sunshine

It's clear that the poet loves Little Herman. Why? Little Herman is filled with so much joy that he seems to turn on the sun! Write about someone who has brought sunshine into your life. The person might be your mother, father, sister, brother, aunt, uncle, niece, nephew, friend, teacher, or anyone else special in your life. Create a poem or a drawing if you'd like.

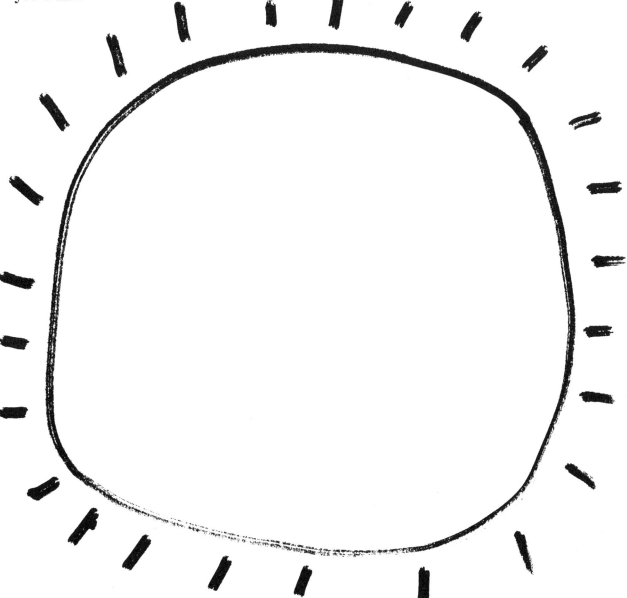

Daddy's Little Girl

I'm my daddy's little girl.
My daddy told me he borrowed
a little piece of sun,
waited until it cooled,
then made me just the way he wanted me . . .
looking like him . . .
(with a little bit of mommy added).
That sun he borrowed is why
my face lights up, so bright when I smile,
and why all of me is so sunshiny.

My girlfriend says she's her daddy's little girl.
Her daddy told her he cut her out
of some midnight,
with a cookie cutter he got from her mommy.
He cut her out of midnight,
because that's his favorite most fun time.
That's why she is all of his happiness . . .
especially when she smiles,
letting the moon shine,
and the stars flash across her face.

My other girlfriend says she's her daddy's little girl.
Her daddy told her that he calls her Honey,
because one day he had a sweet tooth.
So, he and her mommy
gathered up all the flowers they could
and gave those flowers to a whole lot
of worker bees.

Those bees buzzed around . . .
. . . and buzzed around . . .
until they designed her sweet enough
to fill his tooth with her honey drop kiss . . .
fill his heart with her honey shined face . . .
and fill his life with her honeycomb smile.

So, my girlfriends and I decided,
our daddies sure went to a lot of trouble
to make us their little girls.
We guess that's why we love them so much.
Thank you God . . . and mommies
for helping them out.
You know how much we love you, too!

Love Makes a Family

There are many kinds of families. Your family might be like the ones in the poem. Or it might be very different. But every family is held together with love.

Complete this "family album" to tell about your family and share what you think makes a loving family.

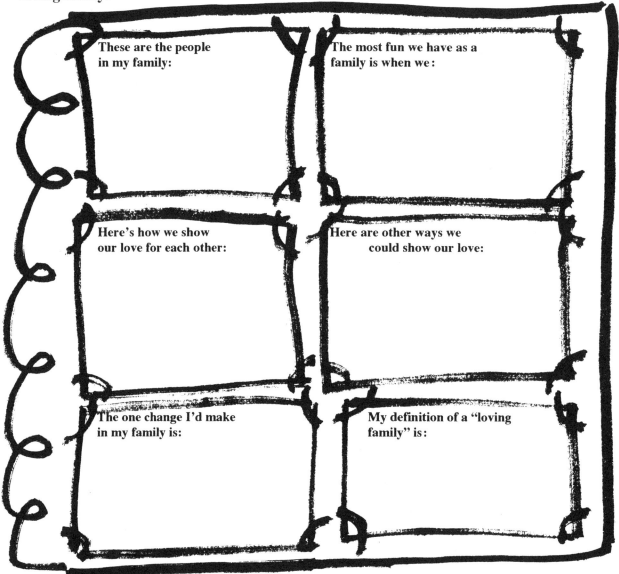

These are the people in my family:

The most fun we have as a family is when we:

Here's how we show our love for each other:

Here are other ways we could show our love:

The one change I'd make in my family is:

My definition of a "loving family" is:

Recipe for Love

Would you like to have your own children someday? What would you do to raise a happy child like the one in the poem? Write your "recipe" for how to love and care for a child.

Recipe for Raising a Happy Child

Ingredients: (check as many as you wish)

Love	Understanding
Patience	Playfulness
Discipline	Togetherness

Other Important Ingredients:

Directions for Raising a Happy Child:

1.

2.

3.

4.

5.

Loving words I'd say to my child every day:

Hugs and Kisses

Hugs and hugs and kisses...
Doesn't she know that I'm a boy ?
Hugs and hugs and kisses...
I'm not some cuddly toy.

Hugs and hugs and kisses...
Boys should be treated rough,
Hugs and hugs and kisses...
These muscles show I'm tough.

Hugs and hugs and kisses...
Makes me want to run and hide.
I can't show the world how warm...
hugs and hugs and kisses...
make me feel
inside.

GirlStuff! BoyStuff!

The boy in the poem thinks there are some things only girls do and some things only boys do. What do you think?

List some things you think are just for girls.

GirlStuff!

Draw some of your ideas if you like.

List some things you think are just for boys.

BoyStuff!

Share your lists with a few people. Discuss what you've written and what they've written. Then look back at your lists. Have you changed your mind about anything? If so, draw a line through anything you want off your list. Or add new things to your list. Then tell what you feel about girl stuff and boy stuff by writing a poem or a song or a play! If you'd like, draw a picture or a cartoon or a doodle!

I'LL TRY

I'll try to think while I am learning,
and not just answer "yes".
I can't become truly smart
if I thoughtlessly guess.

I'll try to always smile,
even when I am feeling sadness.
Maybe my smile will help
someone else feel gladness.

I'll try to go through each day
with these two things in mind . . .
Think and be thoughtful.
Love and be kind.

GROWING EQUATION

Growing + up does not = growing tall.
You can grow up without growing at all.
Your mind is what grows.
(Though it seems the same size.)
Keep it growing and you'll
grow up WISE!

Life Equations

The poems "I'll Try" and "Growing Equations" give good advice about learning and living. For example, the poet uses this "math equation":

Growing + up does not = growing tall

Express your own thoughts about the ideas below. Write equations, sentences, or poems to tell what you think.

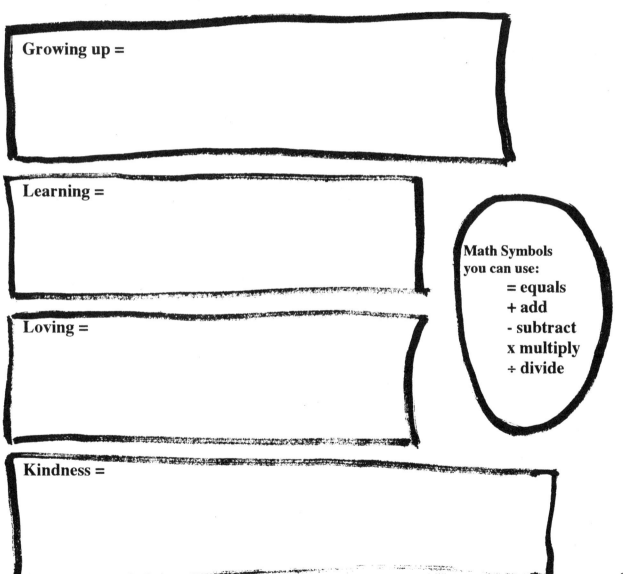

Growing up =

Learning =

Loving =

Math Symbols
you can use:
= equals
+ add
- subtract
x multiply
÷ divide

Kindness =

65

ON A LIMB

"I want to be ripe and round and red,"
the little green apple always said.
For every day he'd see
another apple fall from the tree.
He'd shout, looking down from his tiny limb,
"I want to be big, just like him!"

Each and every day
the other fruit would say,
"Don't be in a hurry to grow so fast,
because the future soon becomes the past."

But, he'd watch the apples every morn,
wondering which one would be gone,
hoping and wishing for his turn.
The little green apple didn't learn,
not to be in a hurry to grow so fast,
because the future soon becomes the past.

At every chance, he'd make
his tiny twig rock and shake,
so more quickly he might be found
on the green and grassy ground.

He was getting bigger and redder
by the day.
As he grew the fruit would say,
"Don't shake your twig. Don't grow so fast.
because the future soon becomes the past."

But he gave another **giant shake**
and the tiny twig…
began to break.
With a bump…
      and a bounce…
         he found
himself laying on the autumn ground.

A little boy looked under the tree
and picked up the apple happily.
Holding the apple very tight…
the little boy took a bite.

The apple finally knew that
what the fruit had said was true.
He was red and ripe and round, at last,
but the future,
too soon, had become the past.

Now he'd give anything to be,
again, a part of his long lost tree.
He looked up,
so that he might find,
a part of what he had left behind.

Before the little boy ate him away,
he heard a little green apple say,
while up high, on a limb,
"I want to be big…
      …just…
        …like…
          …him!"

Talking to an Apple

*"Don't be in a hurry to grow so fast,
because the future soon becomes the past."*

This is the advice one apple gives to the little green apple in the poem. Do you think the little green apple should have followed the advice? Why or why not?

If you had been the little green apple, would you have taken the advice? Why or why not?

What advice would <u>you</u> have given to the little green apple?

68

Talking to Yourself

*"Don't be in a hurry to grow so fast,
because the future soon becomes the past."*

**If you follow this advice, do you think you will
live a better life? Why or why not?**

**Do you know someone who is in too much of
a hurry to grow up? What is that person doing
to grow up too fast? What advice would you
give him or her?**

JUST PUSH

One day the teacher walked us to the
room.
The door was closed, the keys inside.
The teacher tried the door,
but it didn't open.
We waited until he got another key.
That's when he realized
it was open all along.
All he had to do was push.

Sometimes,
I think he does us the same way.
Has us waiting,
while he looks for the key of knowledge,
to let us in,
when really, all he has to do
is give us a little push
by just thinking . . .
we can.

My Key to Knowledge

What do you need to learn at your best? Express your ideas in your own personal key to knowledge.

My Personal Key to Knowledge

Here's what I could do to be a better student:

Here's how my teacher can help me be a better student:

Here's how my family could help me be a better student:

Share your key of knowledge with your teacher and family.

71

GHETTO-ITES

They call our home a ghetto.
They name us worthless ghetto-ites.
They say we stalk the streets and steal,
spreading fear through starless nights.

But...
We live together and learn.
There is strength when we unite.
"Strength in knowledge" is our motto.
We don't waste the time to fight.

Talking about "your momma"
is a game that we don't need.
We're learning about ourselves
            and others,
how to think, compute, and read.

They call our home a ghetto.
So ghetto-ites watch us with pride.
When we stand, we stand up tall,
and when we walk, we S T R U T, we *glide*.
Watch us move.

de bop   de bop!

Ghetto-ites
living... learning... loving...
NON-STOP!!!

Pride Poem

Read this Pride Poem.

> <u>K</u>eeping the promise of Dr. Martin Luther King, Jr.
> <u>E</u>ver ready to help others achieve their dreams
> <u>V</u>ery proud of being who I am
> <u>I</u>nterested in improving myself whenever I can
> <u>N</u>ever afraid to stand up and be heard

Notice that when you add up the first letter of each line, it spells a boy's name—Kevin. Create your own Pride Poem. In the Pride Place, write your name down the left side. Then write a phrase for each line that proudly tells who you are or who you want to be.

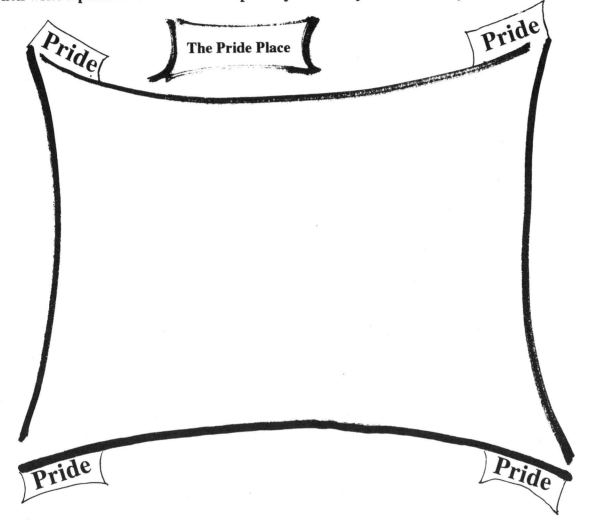

The Pride Place

HOMESICK

(Harold's Poem)

I don't know why we had to move so far
to a house that's only regular,
like the ones in books and on TV
'cause "the projects" was my regular house,
with a lot more neighbors
and ten mothers and fathers
and parties that danced into the halls
so all I had to do was open the door
and I was there.

I don't know why we had to move so far
to a house that's only regular
'cause even outside was better in the projects.
We could stay out real late on Saturdays
and everyday in the summer,
and run relay races and play basketball
or play games and just laugh,
'cause no matter where you went…
your mother or somebody's mother
could always see you
and call you from the windows.

I just don't know why we had to move so far
to a house that's only regular
'cause inside was just as good as outside
in the projects

Only inside was VERTICAL instead of HORIZONTAL.
So I could be a pilot
and make parachutes from rags
and watch them drift down to the street...
or I was the KING
and could see all my subjects
from the tower in the sky...

and when I wanted to protect the world
I'd run up and down the steps
and be a firefighter saving people...

or sometimes I'd just walk across the hall,
and make a special delivery to my friend's house,
where there was always something good
cooking through the door.

I still don't know why we had to move so far,
from someplace special to no place in particular.
'Cause going all the way to this house
took over one hundred years by train
and even though my father was a conductor
it still took forever.

And when we finally got to this
regular house
with white white shingles
and green green grass
there was nobody there who even knew
who I was.

Advice for Harold

Imagine you write an advice column for your local newspaper—like Dear Abby. Write advice for Harold—the boy in the poem who moved from the city to the suburbs. Share your own experiences with him.

Speaking My Mind!

An advice column written by _____
your name

Dear Harold,
Here are some ideas for getting involved in your new community:

Here are some ideas for making new friends:

Imagination Station

In the poem, Harold has some practical fantasies about being a pilot, a firefighter, and a special delivery person. He also has some wild fantasies about being a KING! Enter the Imagination Station. Express your own fantasies about what you might be or do! You can write poems or draw pictures if you like.

77

Halloween Madness

It was already Halloween,
not a witch or black cat was seen.
Not a hoot or frightening scream,
to awaken the night's wicked dream.

No one to trick. No one to treat.
No one even walked the street.
We candy catchers really feared
Halloween had disappeared.

All of a sudden, riding a motor bike,
flew a white cat yowling about a witches' strike.
"All ghostly groups are boycotting, too.
They don't want to become witches' brew."

Of all the tales we'd ever heard,
a witches' strike seemed most absurd.
Until in a sudden, out of the black,
flew CoCo the witch, and her witchly pack.

Thirteen witches made an unusual sight.
Thirteen witches on this Halloween night.
Each held a giant sign on a giant stick,
which read:
WITCHES UNITE AND DO IT QUICK!

Each witch wore her colorful best,
reds, blues and greens for their protest.
They flew around on new vacuum cleaners.

They didn't look at all like Halloweeners.

CoCo spoke. Her voice wasn't fright'ning.
But her words felt like bolts of lightning.
"Stop expecting us to look exactly the same.
We're not all ugly with a horrible frame."

"Look at our faces," was another's retort,
"tell us how many of us have a wart?
Here are our noses, take a look.
How many are long and have a hook?

"Our hair isn't like straw, worn down our back.
And we wear other colors as well as black.
And most of us wouldn't be caught dead
with a tall, pointed hat stuck on our head."

"And," said CoCo, doing some lively prances,
"we Halloween queens do happy dances.
We don't just sing sad songs to the moon
Our magic is sung to the latest tune."

Everyone listened carefully and was quiet,
for many feared a witches' riot.
Few knew exactly what to expect.
But all the witches wanted was some respect.

CoCo's final words to the Halloweeners
were heard over restarting vacuum cleaners.
"Everyone in any group is never exactly alike."
And that was the end of the witches' strike.

The Beauty of Differences

"Everyone in any group is never exactly alike."

Think about this quotation from the poem. Then complete the chart.

Groups I Belong To	How Members in the Group Are Different in Good Ways
My family	
My group of of friends	

Blackness Is...

Blackness is more than the kind of hair,
how dark you are, or what you wear.

It's more than talking about being proud,
or speaking Blackness . . . extra loud.

It's more than what we've never had,
being militant or proving yourself "bad".

It's more than being last, being late,
or being called second rate.

It's more than Black blocks owned by Whites.
It's even more than civil rights.

It's more than acting out a role.
It's even more than having soul.
It's more than a Black community.
Blackness is our unity.

Blackness is how, what, why we feel.
Blackness is love and being for real.
Blackness is what our people do.
Blackness is a beauty you have in you.

Illustration based on original drawing by Keith J. Elam

The Beauty in Me

Look into the mirror of your true self. What beauties do you find there? Write what you see in your mirror. Don't be shy. Praise what you know is there and what others may not yet have seen! You can write a poem or a draw picture if you like.

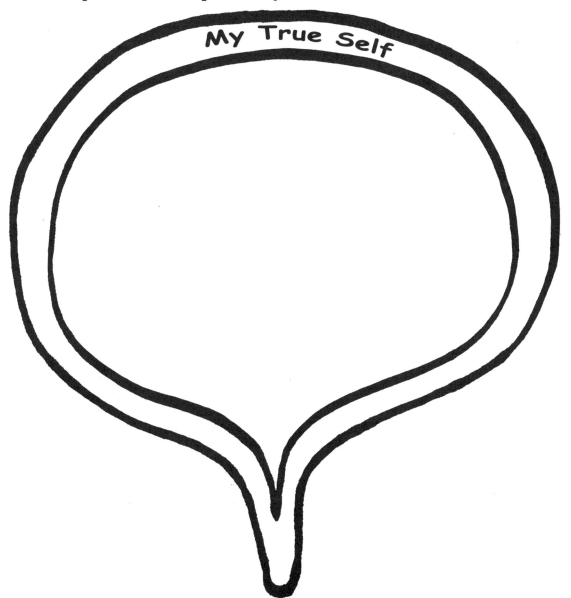

My True Self

Poetry Is Me

A word is what I've lived,
and changes as I live it.
A word really only lives
from the meanings that I give it.

A dictionary can't grab it
and say "Now, this is it."
It gives a place for me to start.
I add myself on my first visit.

With all the probabilities,
I add the possibility
that makes each word belong
and bring meaning to me.

Even my own meanings change.
Sometimes it changes in mid book.
It sometimes changes in mid sentence,
as I give my world another look.

A word is me.
It's what I feel and taste
and touch and smell
and see.

When all the words connect…
just right —
that's poetry.

Wonder Word

Is there a word you think is weird, beautiful, funny, or just plain wonderful? Write it in the star. Then answer the questions about it.

What is special for you about this word?

What is the dictionary definition of the word?

What is <u>your</u> definition of it?

Do you like the <u>sound</u> of your word? Why or why not?

Do you like the <u>look</u> of your word? Why or why not?

If your word could speak, what would it say about itself?

Your <u>name</u> is also a word. Write it in the second star. Then answer the questions about it.

What is special to you about your own name?

Do you like the <u>sound</u> of your name? Why or why not?

Do you like the <u>look</u> of your name? Why or why not?

85

STRANDED...
MAROONED

An idea is bouncing
around in my head,
but I think the words
are lost, or dead . . .

Snagged on a flying rug . . .
lost over ancient Siam . . .
stopped at a broken red light . . .
stuck in an air-traffic jam . . .

Are my words sidetracked
on the other side of the moon?
Are they sky-jacked,
or stranded somewhere marooned?

What can I do with
this great idea,
if the words I want
refuse to appear?

I can't even save it.
No words hold its place.
Where the idea is
will be an empty space.

Is that them "over the river"'
trying to sneak past?
When they get "through the woods"
I'm going to write them down
fast!!!

The Other Side of the Moon

Do you sometimes feel like the poet—as if it's hard to get your thoughts out on paper? Everybody feels that way sometimes. One way even great writers get over the feeling of being "stranded and marooned" is to "**freewrite**."

You can find out what that is right now! Put your pencil or pen at the top of the moon. Then begin to write ANYTHING and DON'T STOP. You may start out by writing "moon, moon, moon" over and over. Or you might start out by writing "I don't know what to write." It doesn't matter. Just keep words flowing out of your pen or pencil onto the other side of the moon—for five minutes! Ready, set, go to the moon!

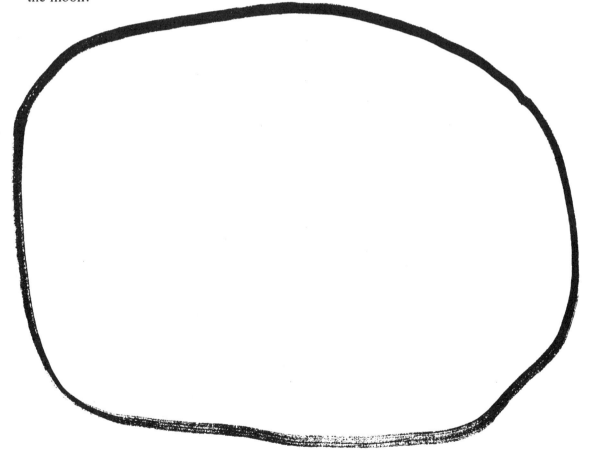

 Were you surprised by any of the thoughts that flowed out of you during your freewriting?

IDEA SITTING

Some people write
and they're through with it,
but when I write, I write and sit.

I write . . . cross out . . . put in
some more
And when I'm finished . . . finally . . .
for sure . . .

I sit back, ideas down and done.
Then out of the air pops another one.

IN OTHER WORDS

I know, I know. "Fasten my lip."
Will somebody give me a paper clip?

Not strong enough!
I need a safety pin . . .
to fasten all that happens

in.
I'll "button it up."
O.K. O.K.!
It will never fit into one day.

But if there's a pencil I can borrow,
I'll write a reminder for tomorrow.

Pick Up Your Pencil!

Write about three things you've been thinking about or feeling lately. It doesn't matter what the ideas are. They might be something silly or something serious. Jot down your thoughts and feelings as quickly as you can.

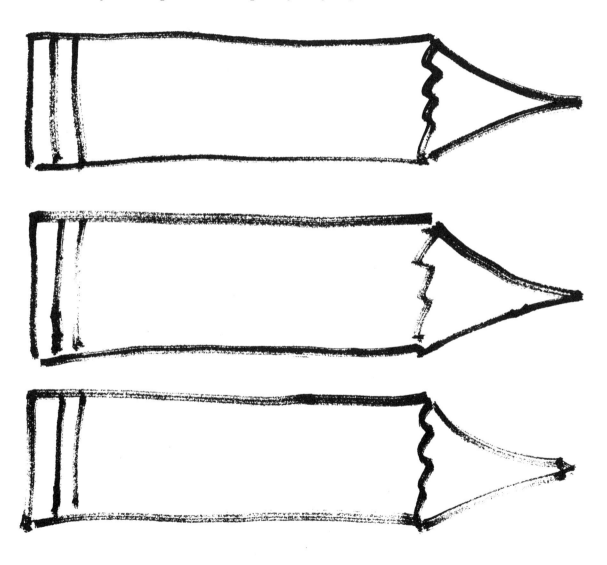

Save your writing. Come back to it another day. Choose one idea to develop more completely into a longer paragraph, a poem, a song, a drawing or anything else you'd like.

SPELLING BLUES

Added lyrics
on audio
version.

I'll tell you something, but please don't tell.
I can write and I can read, but I cannot spell.

I look at the words on pages, then close my eyes.
There must be millions of words to memorize.

I write poems and stories
and mess up my penmanship.
The teacher might miss my mistakes,
if I let my pencil slip.

I usually play it safe, and switch the words I use.
The words I can spell, are the words I choose.

I refuse to write on the board
in front of the class.
I have night and day-mares
about spelling tests I can't pass.

I really need some help.
I'm going gradually insane.
Yesterday, I wrote my heading
and mispelled my own last name.

It's a serious condition.
I'm going to report it to the news.
I think I'm going to call it
the "I Cant Spel Blews"

I'll probably get arrested
for... RAMPANT SPELLING ABUSE.
I can hear my sentence now,
LIFE FOR ALPHABET MISUSE.

Sing Out!

Write words for a song. Let the first part of the song tell about something you don't do as well as you like. Let the second part of the song tell about how you could improve. Use the tune of a song you know. Here's a short example:

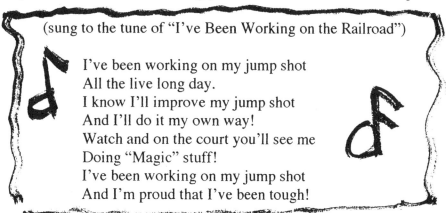

(sung to the tune of "I've Been Working on the Railroad")

I've been working on my jump shot
All the live long day.
I know I'll improve my jump shot
And I'll do it my own way!
Watch and on the court you'll see me
Doing "Magic" stuff!
I've been working on my jump shot
And I'm proud that I've been tough!

A WORLD TO READ

We are needing…
a world of reading.

Help us get a wondrous start.
Feed our minds…our souls… our hearts.
Fill us with language as we mature.
Read to us much much more.

We are needing…
a world of reading.

Give us something we can never lose…
Something money can't buy,
that we'll always use.
Thoughts to excite our imagination…
Books to inspire us — the new generation.

We are needing…
a world of reading.

Bring the universe to our door.
Teach us to open it and explore.
If the whole world is a stage,
show us how to play each page.

What we are needing is
a whole world of reading.

Opening Doors

Reading can open doors to the world! Books can tell you what you want to know and how to do something. They can even offer you tips on how to become the person you want to be! Write what you would like to read about in the "doors" below.

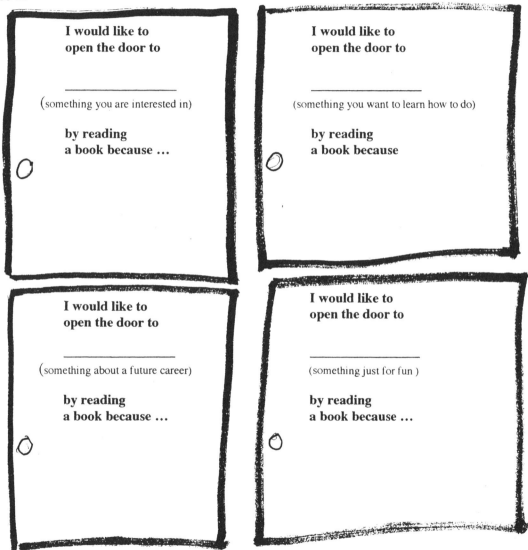

**I would like to
open the door to**

_____

(something you are interested in)

**by reading
a book because ...**

**I would like to
open the door to**

_____

(something you want to learn how to do)

**by reading
a book because**

**I would like to
open the door to**

_____

(something about a future career)

**by reading
a book because ...**

**I would like to
open the door to**

_____

(something just for fun)

**by reading
a book because ...**

Ask your teacher or a librarian to help you find the books you want to open doors in your own life.

Much, Much More...

This book may look
like it's come to the end,
but if poetry really
has become your friend,
you'll read more and more and more...
and then...
you'll want to pick up your pencil
or pen
and **poetize** yourself.

I Am A Poem!

Put your hand down on this page and draw an outline of it. Then in the outline of your hand, write a poem about yourself.

Tell what you are like or what you hope to be someday or anything else you'd like to express about yourself. Celebrate yourself—you are a poem of joy! Remember your poem doesn't have to rhyme and it can have drawings or decorations or anything you like.

Poetic License

To be presented as needed.

The bearer is officially author / ized to: arrange, change, invent, improvise, regroup, rhyme or unrhyme any and all words, phrases, sentences and fragments -- for the purpose of painting pictures in the hearts, minds and souls of all -- in order to express thoughts, feelings, emotions and the truth as the bearer sees it . . . in the most original and creative style.

X _____

Author / izing signature
Sign your own name. Only *you* can grant yourself this license.

_____

Witness to creativity
Lindamichellebaron